This
Hannah Montana
Annual belongs to

Nicole McLeod ....

My top three Hannah
Montana songs are

1 *Rockstar* ....
2 *Best of Both worlds* ....
3 *Nobodys Perfect* ....

DISNEY

HANNAH MONTANA

ANNUAL 2009

EGMONT

We bring stories to life

First published in Great Britain 2009
by Egmont UK Limited,
239 Kensington High Street, London W8 6SA.
© Disney Enterprises, Inc.
Based on the series created by Michael Poryes & Rich Correll & Barry O'Brien

Editor: Rennie Brown
Designer: Laura Bird

ISBN 978 1 4052 4292 9
3 5 7 9 10 8 6 4 2
Printed in Italy.

All Rights Reserved.

what's

8   All about Miley

10   All about Lilly

12   All about Oliver

14   Miley's family

16   Jackson alert

17   Funky fours

18   Secret status

20   Sketch sudoku

21   My secret album

26   Celebrity ID

28   Poster power

30   Popstar party

32   Party invitations

34   Memory game

37   Studio sound

38   Miley style

40   Hannah style

inside

42 Star makeover

44 Pop performance

45 Hanging out!

46 Lilly's stars

48 So embarrassing

50 Miley's world

51 Matching pair

52 Backstage pass

54 Reversible bag

56 Criss cross

57 Guitar crazy

58 Friends forever

60 Friendship style

62 Rock and rule!

63 Nail art

64 Quiz time

66 Puzzle answers

All about Miley

She may look like an ordinary teen, but Miley's a girl with a BIG secret...

NAME: Miley Stewart

LIVES: In a cool beach-front house in Malibu.

BEST FRIENDS: Lilly and Oliver.

WORST ENEMIES: Ashley and Amber.

PERSONALITY PROFILE: Miley's the one and only Hannah Montana! But only those close to her know her secret ID! Shhh!

Secret POP STAR

ONE TIME...

When celebrity, Jake Ryan, first started going to Seaview Middle School, Miley was a bit jealous of all the special treatment he got! She decided that her life might be a bit more fun if everybody knew she was famous! Big, big mistake!

As soon as she'd revealed her secret identity to a newspaper reporter, Miley had a massive attack of regret! When the reporter came round to her house, quick-thinking Miley got dressed up in a crazy costume and sang out of tune. It was her most un-Hannahish performance ever! The reporter decided that she was just a crazy impostor and Miley's secret stayed safe! Phew!

Fill in your own Miley profile!

My favourite thing about Miley is.....That at night
She can become hannah Montana......

....

....

If we were friends I'd like to.....Have a V.I.P
ticket to all of her Concerts...

....

....

WORD UP

Circle the words that best describe Miley.

CUTE   CRAZY   SWEET

FUNNY   KIND

LOYAL

SPORTY   MUSICAL

TALENTED

AMAZING   SHOW OFF

9

All about Lilly

She's smart, she's sassy and she's never far away when Miley needs a friend! Go, Lilly!

NAME: Lilly Truscott

LIVES: Not far from Miley's house.

BEST FRIENDS: Miley and Oliver.

WORST ENEMIES: Ashley and Amber.

PERSONALITY PROFILE: Lilly is an ace skateboarder and a bit of a tomboy. She's a good listener and a great friend to have around.

ONE TIME...

Lilly wanted to give her mum something special, so she decided to record her a song. But Lilly's not such a great singer and the song sounded awful! Miley decided to give her friend some professional help and secretly edited Lilly's terrible track. When Lilly heard the new and improved version of her song, she decided to unleash her, er, 'talent' on the world! Before Miley could stop her, Lilly agreed to compete against Amber in a karaoke contest! It looked like Lilly was in for a disastrous night, until Miley 'fessed up. Together, they came up with a plan, so Lilly wasn't humiliated. What a team!

Fill in your own Lilly profile!

My favourite thing about Lilly is... Shes very funny
And is exciteble

If we were friends I'd like to... Watch her
Skateboarding tricks

All about Oliver

When the going gets tough, Oliver's the kind of guy you want around. He wouldn't dream of quitting on his friends.

NAME: Oliver Oken

LIVES: In the same town as Miley.

BEST FRIENDS: Miley and Lilly.

WORST ENEMIES: Ashley and Amber.

PERSONALITY PROFILE: If there's a job to be done, Oliver will follow it through, no matter what! He believes that he can do anything, as long as he tries hard! He's a loyal and trustworthy friend.

ONE TIME...

Back before Oliver knew the truth about Miley's secret identity, he had a not-so-secret crush on Hannah Montana! He was her number one fan. In fact, he couldn't stop thinking about her! He even helped Lilly break into Hannah's dressing room after a concert one night! But when Oliver tried to get into Hannah's limo, Miley and Lilly realised that his crush was way, wa-ay, out of hand! Something had to be done! So Miley disguised herself in popstar clothes and acted majorly gross to put Oliver off Hannah for good!

Fill in your own Oliver profile!

My favourite thing about Oliver is..

....

....

....

If we were friends I'd like to...

....

....

....

WORD UP
Circle the words that best describe Oliver.

CUTE   SWEET

CRAZY   LOYAL

FUNNY   KIND

COOL   MUSICAL

TALENTED

AMAZING   DETERMINED

13

Miley's family

They're cool, they're crazy, they're Miley's family!

NAME: Robby Stewart

LIVES: With his two children, Miley and Jackson.

BEST POINT: He's totally understanding... most of the time.

WORST POINT: He can be pretty strict when it comes to school work.

PERSONALITY PROFILE: As well as being a great dad, Robby is also a pretty good singer - no wonder Miley is so talented!

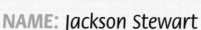

NAME: Jackson Stewart

LIVES: With his dad and his sister.

BEST POINT: He's full of crazy ideas and he's always playing practical jokes.

WORST POINT: He can be totally annoying!

PERSONALITY PROFILE: Jackson's got a zany sense of humour and he's pretty good at getting his own way, too!

Fill in your own Stewart family profile!

My favourite thing about Miley's family is...

....

....

....

If I could live with the Stewarts for one week I would.............................

....

....

....

....

....

....

....

....

Jackson alert

Is there anything more annoying than an annoying brother?
Probably not! Find the Jackson-related words in the search!

```
Y  I  E  R  O  P  L  D  W  O  R  C
E  S  F  L  R  T  O  L  E  N  R  Y
N  S  E  S  I  B  U  F  G  A  N  G
O  R  O  T  N  B  D  N  Z  H  O  N
M  E  E  F  O  P  O  Y  G  E  H  I
T  H  I  H  A  M  G  M  I  E  P  Y
E  C  O  C  T  H  E  O  K  T  O  O
K  U  N  I  L  O  O  R  L  O  R  N
C  A  S  T  S  S  R  G  V  E  C  N
O  R  O  A  A  L  A  B  E  T  I  A
P  K  C  A  T  T  A  K  C  A  N  S
S  K  C  O  S  Y  L  L  E  M  S  R
```

Words can run forwards, backwards and diagonally!

Words to find

SMELLY SOCKS
LOUD
TV REMOTE
SOFA HOG
CRAZY

POCKET MONEY
SNACK ATTACK
MOBILE
ANNOYING
BROTHER

 16

Turn to page 66 for the answers.

Funky fours

All the clues below have four-letter answers. Write your answers in the grid, then unscramble the letters in the pink boxes to reveal a secret word!

Turn to page 66 for the answers.

1. Engagement _ _ _ _
2. _ _ _ _ _ skirt
3. _ _ _ _ _ brush
4. Clothes _ _ _ _

5. Pop _ _ _ _ _
6. Home _ _ _ _ _
7. _ _ _ _ _ fight
8. _ _ _ _ _ up

THE MYSTERY
WORD IS...

Secret status

How do you handle secrets? Take this quiz to find out!

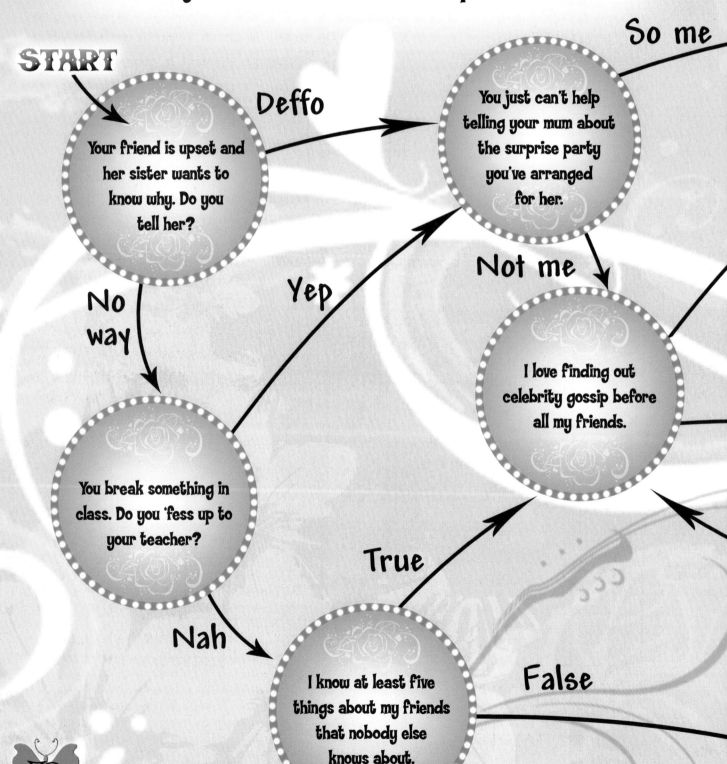

START

Your friend is upset and her sister wants to know why. Do you tell her?

Deffo

You just can't help telling your mum about the surprise party you've arranged for her.

So me

No way

You break something in class. Do you 'fess up to your teacher?

Yep

Not me

I love finding out celebrity gossip before all my friends.

True

Nah

I know at least five things about my friends that nobody else knows about.

False

I'm not into whispering. I'd rather get everything out in the open.

So Me

Not Me

SECRET SHARER

Whispering and passing notes is not what you're about! You'd rather it was all out in the open! For you, telling the truth is much more important than keeping secrets. But don't tell the world about your big brother's teddy or the name of your best friend's crush! Try to hold back just a teensy bit!

secret star

So me

Not me

Keeping secrets is more important than anything else.

No

SECRET SORTER

There are some things you can't keep to yourself because you know it's best to speak up. And there are other secrets you guard with your life! Luckily, you know exactly when to 'fess up and when to keep zipped! You're totally sorted when it comes to secrets. You've got the balance just right!

Yep

Nah

Deffo

I tell my best friend everything - including everybody's secrets.

SECRET SAVER

You've totally earned the trust and respect your friends give to you. A secret is a secret - simple as! You wouldn't spill for anyone or anything! Being a trustworthy friend means a lot, but remember that it's sometimes okay to share secrets, especially if a friend is in trouble! Speak up if you need to!

Sketch suduko

Grab your pencils and get arty
with this sketchy sudoku!
Complete the grid so each icon
only appears once
in each row and column.

Draw the
missing icons
in the blank
spaces!

Turn to page 66 for the answers.

20

My secret album

"Hi, y'all! Miley here! If you promise not to tell anyone about my true identity, you can take a peek at my secret album!"

Talk about a bad hair day! Lucky I wear a wig when I'm performing as Hannah Montana!

I guess covering your head with a hat, is a good way of hiding bad hair. But this is soo not my style!

There are some things that just shouldn't be kept in lockers!

What can I say? He annoyed me. He deserved it. He's Jackson.

Lilly's the kind of friend I used to wish on a star for. I'm so glad she's in my life.

Being a popstar is not all about the glamour, especially if you are related to my brother!

Okay, so this was very wrong. But when you've accidentally recorded yourself talking about your crush, you HAVE to get the tape back!

When I dance people just can't help joining in! Ha! Ha! Somehow I don't think this routine will make it on stage!

Me and Lilly hitting the shops.
Happy days!

We'll always be best friends –
whatever disguises we wear!

My dad always manages to cheer
me up! It's kinda good to have him
around... er, unless he's telling one
of his Uncle Earl stories, that is!

When Jackson isn't being
completely annoying, he's kind of
fun to have around! Just don't tell
him I said that!

Here I am reading to a bunch of little kids. Aren't they cute?

I love singing with my dad. He's the best songwriter a girl could have!

I love singing with my dad. He's the best songwriter a girl could have!

Celebrity ID

**If you were famous, what kind of celeb would you be?
Find out with this quiz!**

If my life was a movie it would be...
a. All about me.
b. About my friends.
c. A mega musical.

If I was a dog I'd be...
a. A chihuahua.
b. The leader of the pack.
c. A top barker.

I love dressing like my friends.
a. Uh-uh! I set the trends!
b. Sure. It's fun to co-ordinate.
c. I do my own thing.

I would like my fave flowers...

a. Sent to me by adoring fans.

b. In my band's dressing room.

c. Painted on my private tour bus.

I love having my picture taken...

a. When I'm looking my very best!

b. With my best friends.

c. Posing with my microphone.

What would be your top present?

a. Your own DVD player.

b. A day out with the girls.

c. A gorgeous guitar.

I am always humming...

a. The theme of my fave film.

b. To my friends.

c. Tunes I've written myself.

Mainly A's

Watch out, Hollywood, there's a new starlet on the horizon! You've got the right 'tude to make it big on the silver screen! Your drama diva ways and acting talent will be sure to stun the crowds!

Mainly B's

Rev up the tour bus! You were made to be in a world-famous girl band! Hanging out with a group of pals 24/7 is your idea of a good time! You'd love sharing the spotlight with your friends!

Mainly C's

With your dedication and musical talent, a solo singing career is the only way forward! You'd rock out in front of crowds all over the world! Are you ready to see your name in lights?

Poster power

Design a poster for Hannah's next concert. Make sure you draw yourself some front row tickets, too!

Get inspired

Use Hannah's favourite designs on your poster and she's sure to love it! Try these out!

Draw your front row tickets here!

HANNAH MONTANA live in concert

Friday Night 8.00 - 10.00

Hannah Montana

Live In Concert.

Friday night
8.00 - 10.00

Signed Pics - 1.00
C.DS - 10.00
Posters - 3.00
Calenders - 5.00
Glowsticks - 1.00
glow braclets
4 for £1.00

Popstar party

Snacks, sounds and crazy games! We've got everything you need to get your party started!

VIP Snacks

Make your mates feel like VIPs by serving up some star-worthy snacks! Delicious dips, with pitta bread and carrot sticks are great savoury nibbles and cheesy wedges are always a big hit! For a delicious desert, try pushing sliced fruit and marshmallows onto a kebab stick. Fruit kebabs look amazing and they're totally easy to make!

Star in the Spotlight

This is the perfect game to play in the dark! Ask everyone to sit in a circle, turn out the lights and get a torch. Spin the torch in the middle of the circle and wait for it to stop. The person in the spotlight has to sing her favourite Hannah Montana song as loudly as she can! Keep spinning the torch until everyone in the group has had a turn in the spotlight!

Turn it up!

Organise your CD collection before your party, so you don't have to search around for your fave Hannah Montana soundtrack! On the night, you could ask everyone to take turns at being the DJ. Make up funky DJ names for each other, if you like! DJs get to pick all their fave music, while everyone else gets down to some serious dancing!

Funky forfeits

Ask everyone to write three crazy forfeits on different scraps of paper. The only rule is that all the forfeits must be safe to do indoors! Oh, and don't write a forfeit that you wouldn't do yourself, 'cos you might end up doing it later! Put all the forfeits in a hat, close your eyes and pick one out. The person with the most embarrassing forfeit goes first!

Party

Get your party off to a rockin' start with these funky invitations. They're totally star-studded!

What you need:
* ★ Purple card
* ★ Safety scissors
* ★ Pink paper
* ★ Yellow card
* ★ Glue stick
* ★ Pencil

1

Fold the purple card in half to make a greetings card. Now cut a strip from the front of the card. Open up the card and glue the pink paper inside.

invitations

2

Using a faint pencil, draw three star shapes on to the yellow card. When you are happy with them, carefully cut them out with your scissors.

3

Lay your stars face down and dab some glue along one side of each star. Now stick the gluey side on to the front of the card. Once it has dried, you can write your invitation!

Memory game

Do you have a magical memory or are you a total sieve-head?
Play Miley's memory game and find out!

HOW TO PLAY
Set a timer and look at these photos for three minutes. When your time is up, flip over the page to find out what to do next...

35

Memory game

Now take the test to reveal the secrets of your memory.

Out or in?

Which of these items DID appear in Miley's photos?

- Teddy bear
- Concert stage
- Spotty t-shirt
- Pink guitar
- Skateboard
- Black feather
- White feather
- Crazy wig
- Puppy dog
- Video game

Details, details...

Which of these little details didn't appear in Miley's photos?

Colour Crazy

Test your colour memory! What colour was the tent?

a   b   c

What colours were Miley's PJs?

a   b   c

36

Now check the pictures on the previous pages to see how you did!

Studio sound

These pictures may look alike, but there are five differences in picture 2. Time how long it takes you to spot them all!

1.

2.

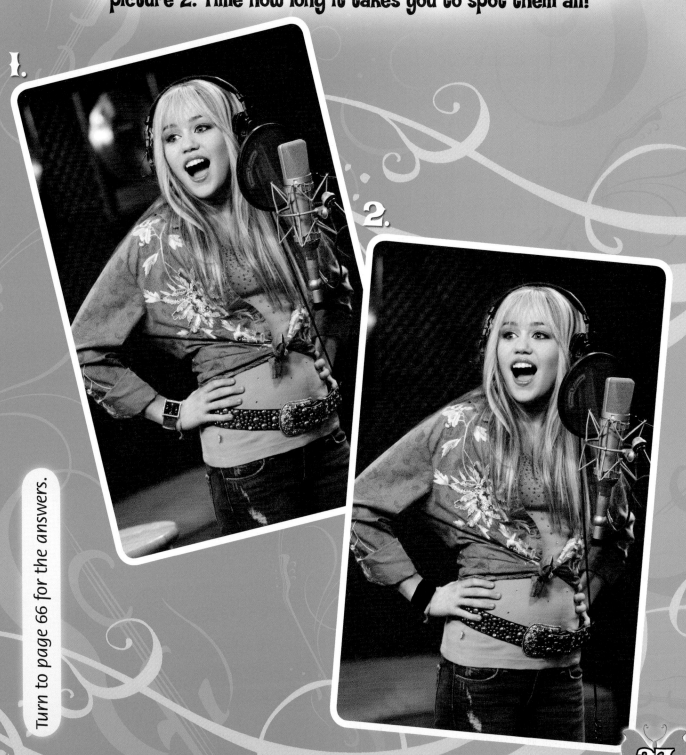

Turn to page 66 for the answers.

37

Miley style

"Hi, y'all! I just know you're mad about fashion, so come and take a peek inside my wardrobe!"

"When it comes to fashion, I'm the exact opposite to my best friend, Lilly. She's a total tomboy! I'm more into girly stuff. I like flowery patterns and embroidered details, but I'm not all about the pink! I have got bright colours in my wardrobe, but I usually match them with browns and greens to tone them down a bit. Being Hannah is totally awesome, but it's nice to dress casual and just be Miley. I guess you could say I've got the best of both wardrobes! Ha! Ha!"

Miley works the layered look!

These shorts are totally trendy!

Funky boots!

Hannah style

"Now it's time to talk fashion, Hannah style! Check out my favourite spotlight-worthy outfits!"

"Leading a double life means I get to have a double wardrobe, too! Seriously, what more could a girl ask for? Well, actually, I'd like a less annoying brother – but, hey, we're supposed to be talking fashion here! So where was I? Oh, yeah, being a secret popstar and having a secret popstar wardrobe is pretty cool. When I'm on stage, I go for loads of denim, sparkly fabrics and funky accessories. If I dress like a star, I sing like a star. Simple as!"

A girl's gotta shine!

Dark denim looks awesome with gold!

Cute heels, Hannah!

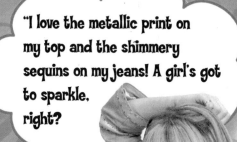

"I love the metallic print on my top and the shimmery sequins on my jeans! A girl's got to sparkle, right?

Printed tees look totally rock!

Hannah works popstar look to the max!

Check out the bling-tastic bangles!

These wedges look great with jeans!

41

Star makeover

Okay y'all! It's makeover time! Follow these top tips and you and your friends will soon shine like stars!

Sparkle and Shine

When Miley changes into Hannah's sparkly clothes, you just know she's going to put on a star performance! Start your makeover by picking out the most dazzling outfit you have. Don't worry if it's not exactly the same as Hannah's - being a star is all about individuality! Look for anything with sparkle - skirts with sequined hems, metallic print t-shirts - what ever you like, as long as it shines!

Get Stylin'

Why not invite some friends over and act as each others stylists! Ask everyone to bring a heap of clothes and hair accessories, so you can try out something new! Take it in turns to invent new hairstyles for each other. Then have a fashion show, wearing your popstar outfits. Get everybody to do a funny microphone pose a-la-hairbrush, then work out some new pop poses to wow the crowds! Cool!

Set up your own photoshoot with your friends and take some funky pictures of your new popstar look!

Feeling shy? Don't panic! Hold your head up and smile to give yourself some star confidence!

Rock Out!

Now it's time to practise your dance routine. Choose your fave Hannah song, mark out a stage area and get ready to groove! Think about how you want to make your entrance. Do you need some dramatic moves or does the song start slowly? Make sure your routine tells a story - just like the song does. Keep on practising and you'll soon be ready for your star performance! Go, girl!

Ask if you can customise some old clothes for your makeover. Fabric glitter paint t-shirts are totally pop!

Sparkly lip gloss and pale eyeshadow is all you need for the Hannah look!

Pop performance

Hannah puts on a star performance every time!
Can you find the concert-related words in this search?

```
M  I  C  R  O  P  H  O  N  E  R  C
T  S  F  A  F  T  C  L  E  N  E  Y
R  R  P  S  E  B  F  H  G  I  N  E
F  E  S  O  N  M  E  N  E  H  O  M
N  E  H  S  T  P  A  H  G  E  H  A
D  H  I  K  T  L  G  F  I  E  R  F
Y  C  T  C  N  E  I  O  K  T  O  S
F  A  N  S  E  T  K  G  L  O  R  P
L  A  S  G  S  S  T  C  H  E  C  I
U  R  A  A  A  L  A  V  I  T  I  N
B  T  E  K  D  W  O  R  C  T  M  G
S  N  A  P  F  R  A  T  I  U  G  R
```

Words can run forwards, backwards and diagonally!

Words to find

SPOTLIGHT
FANS
TICKETS
GUITAR
STAGE

HIT
MICROPHONE
CHEERS
CROWD
FAME

 44

Turn to page 66 for the answers.

Hanging out!

Miley loves hanging out with her friends and family.
Can you spot five differences in picture 2?

1.

2.

Turn to page 66 for the answers.

Lilly's stars

Want to know the secrets of your star-sign element?
Lilly's mystical guide will reveal all!

Fire signs

Aries, Leo and Sagittarius
Personality profile: You're super social and you're always getting told off in class for your chatterbox ways! But just because you talk a lot, doesn't mean you're no good at keeping secrets. You're totally trustworthy when it counts.
Friendship profile: Your friends love your loyalty and your sunshine personality.
Most likely to say: "Want to come to my party?"

Water signs

Cancer, Pisces and Scorpio
Personality profile: You're definitely the arty-type and you've got a real talent for picking out cool clothes and accessories. You always make time for your friends and family and your caring nature means that your pals often come to you for advice.
Friendship profile: You're a good listener and a truly caring mate.
Most likely to say: "Tell me all about it!"

Air signs

Gemini, Libra and Aquarius

Personality profile: You've got a talent for approaching situations differently, which is why you're such a great problem-solver. When you're not masterminding brilliant schemes, you're dreaming up sweet surprises for your pals. Aww, how thoughtful!

Friendship profile: You're a well-respected mate and heaps of fun to be around.

Most likely to say: "Let's look at it in a different way..."

Earth signs

Taurus, Virgo, Capricorn

Personality profile: You're a considerate friend, who notices the little things that other people miss. If a friend's feeling down, you'll pick up on it - even if she's great at hiding her emotions. You're a total star when it comes to practical problems, too!

Friendship profile: You're a down-to-earth friend who's easy to trust.

Most likely to say: "Want to talk about it?"

So embarrassing!

Talk about cringey! My cheeks are still burning from these shameful events!

Ooh-arr me hearties

"Me and Lilly thought it might be pretty cool to be cheerleaders, so we tried out for the cheerleading squad. Lilly was picked for the team and I was picked... as the dorky mascot. I had to dress up in a pirate costume in front of everyone. The shame! The shame! Ooh-arr the shame!"

Ichy-coo

"I went on this camping trip with my class one time and Amber and Ashley were being super annoying. So anyway, me and my friends decided to play a prank on them, but things didn't exactly go to plan... We ended up hiding in a poison oak bush, you know the kind that makes you itch? I couldn't stop scratching myself! I looked like a dog with fleas!"

Spot on

"I was trying to convince Lilly that looks didn't matter, when somebody put a fake zit on a poster of Hannah Montana. Talk about embarrassing! The poster was so big it made the zit look the size of a school bus! Seriously NOT a good look."

Miley's world

Miley's friends and family mean the world to her!
Complete the grid so each person only appears
once in each row and column.

Write their
initials in the
blank spaces!

Turn to page 66 for the answers.

Matching pair

These tickets may look the same, but only two of them match exactly! Are you sharp enough to spot them?

a.

Ticket number 0012524ZP

HANNAH MONTANA

Saturday night at 11pm
London

b.

Ticket number 0012524ZP

HANNAH MONTANA

Saturday night at 11pm
London

c.

Ticket number 0012524ZP

HANNAH MONTANA

Saturday night at 8pm
London

d.

Ticket number 0012524ZP

HANNAH MONTANA

Saturday night at 7pm
London

e.

Ticket number 0012524ZP

HANNAH MONTANA

Saturday night at 8pm
Los Angeles

f.

Ticket number 0012524ZP

HANNAH MONTANA

Saturday night at 8pm
London

Turn to page 66 for the answers.

Backstage pass

Who'll get their hands on the backstage pass to Hannah's concert? Play this game to find out!

START

You will need:
★ A dice.
★ A counter for each player

How to play:
★ Place your counters at the start.
★ Roll the dice to start the game - the highest number goes first.
★ Race your way around the board to see who wins the backstage pass!

You trip over your guitar.
Miss a turn!

Bleugh! Your bro sprays you with stinky aftershave!
Skip a go to wash it off!

You can't find your concert tickets.
Go back to the start!

Uh-oh! Your shoes clash with your top!
Miss a turn!

Hooray! Your cab's here and you're ready to go! **Drive forward one space!**

BACKSTAGE PASS

Name: Leley.o.L.

Stick your photo here

Uh-oh! You've forgotten your jacket. **Go back a space!**

FINISH

Now fill in your pass!

Yay! You've finally arrived! **Finish and collect your backstage pass!**

Sing your fave Hannah Montana song! **Roll the dice again!**

Pull over to grab some snacks for the show. **Go back one!**

Take a short cut to the concert venue! **Go forward one!**

53

Reversible bag

This denim bag has two different sides to suit your mood!

What you need:

★ Old jeans
★ Safety scissors
★ Needle and thread
★ Craft glue
★ Glitter
★ Sequins

To make the bag, cut out both the front and the back of the jean pocket in one piece. Put the pocket aside and cut out the seam from the inside leg of your jeans to make the strap.

2

Put the ends of the strap inside the pocket and ask an adult to stitch it in place with thread. Now you're ready to decorate your reversible bag! Get your glitter *ready, girls!*

3

Use craft glue to draw a flower on one side of the bag then sprinkle glitter over the glue. Wait for it to dry, then draw a glue star on the other side and sprinkle with glitter and sequins.

Criss cross

Fit all the school words into the criss cross below and go to the top of the class!

4 letters	5 letters	6 letters
Note	Lilly	Oliver
Dork	Books	Locker
~~Cool~~	Lunch	~~School~~

7 letters	8 letters	9 letters
Holiday	Homework	Detention
Trouble		

COOL

SCHOOL

Turn to page 66 for the answers.

Guitar crazy

Y'all reckon you've got good eyesight? Count how many guitars are crammed on to this page!

51

Turn to page 66 for the answers.

Friends forever!

"Hey, y'all! Check out my top friendship tips!"

Double trouble

"Having a best friend doesn't mean that you have to be into all the same things. Take me and Lilly for example, I'm totally tuned into music and Lilly is totally out of tune. She a top skater chick and I'm a top sofa surfer. It doesn't matter that we're both into different stuff. In a way, it kind of makes things more interesting. Have you heard the saying opposites attract? Well, when it comes to friendship it's totally true. So don't worry if you guys aren't complete doubles. Just be who you are!"

Keep it real

"You can't always be around each other 24/7. One of you might go on a family holiday or even move to another town. Spending time apart isn't the end of your friendship. You just gotta think of new ways to keep in touch. Stay in contact with texts, emails and letters and you'll keep close no matter what."

Be yourself

"Y'all know the best thing about friendship? Well, I'll tell you right now, friendship isn't about who you know and what you've got - it's about people. People who love hanging out together and helping each other out. When you're with friends, you can be who you are, no questions asked. I love spending time with Lilly and Oliver. Eating snacks in front of the TV, chilling on the beach or hanging backstage. Whatever we do, I can always be myself with them - that's what friendship is all about!"

Work it out

"Okay, so you and your friends aren't always going to agree about everything. You're totally different people, right? If things get off track and you start to argue, take a deep breath and try to see things from each other's point of view. If you keep calm and talk things through you're bound to work things out!"

59

Friendship

What do your friends love about you? Find out with this quiz!

You're out shopping for shampoo. Which one would you buy?

a) Something super expensive. You're worth every penny!
b) A shampoo that's bursting with fruity fragrance.
c) You don't care, as long as it's biodegradable.

If they named a cake after you, what would it be called?

a) Gorgeous gateaux.
b) Fun bun.
c) Melting heart.

What would you rather take to a desert island?

a) Celeb-worthy shades.
b) A beach ball.
c) Your secret journal.

style

Okay, so it's been raining for, like, h-o-u-r-s. What would you do?

a) Have a major makeover sesh.
b) Play forfeits and dares.
c) Settle down for a cosy chat.

A totally cheesy song comes on the radio. What do you do?

a) Roll your eyes and tune in to something more sophisticated.
b) Pull a comedy face and sing along at the top of your voice.
c) Leave it on. It may be dorky, but your best friend loves it!

MOSTLY As Sophisticated honey

There's a bit of magic about you that seems to settle over your friends like fairy dust. You always manage to make them feel gorgeous! You're full of compliments and you're totally ace at makeovers, too! A stylish sort like you is handy to have around!

MOSTLY Bs Sunshine Girl

You always manage to get the group giggling with a hilarious game or a side-splitting joke! You're a total fun magnet and your friends know it! Wherever you are, good times follow! Your pals love hanging out with you, cos you're such a ray of sunshine.

MOSTLY Cs Caring cutie

Wow, you are sweeter than sugar! You're a totally loyal and caring friend and you're a great listener, too! If anybody wants a heart-to-heart chat, they know they can come to you. You always want the best for everyone and everything. You're a true sweetheart!

ROCK AND RULE!

WANT TO KNOW IF YOU FOLLOW THE RULES?
SEE IF YOU CAN OBEY THESE FOUR SIMPLE INSTRUCTIONS!

1. DO NOT THINK OF YOUR FAVOURITE HANNAH MONTANA SONG.
2. DO NOT MOVE YOUR HEAD.
3. DO NOT YAWN, YAWN OR YAWNY-YAWN-YAWN.
4. DO NOT CHECK OUT WHAT'S WRITTEN UPSIDE-DOWN.

REBEL

HOW DID YOU SCORE?

ADD UP THE NUMBER OF RULES YOU DID NOT OBEY. NO CHEATING!

0 = YEAH, RIGHT! YOU ARE SOO NOT TELLING THE TRUTH!
1 = YOU RECKON RULES ROCK. YOUR TEACHERS LOVE YOU!
2 = YOU CAN CONFORM WHEN YOU NEED TO AND THAT'S WHAT COUNTS!
3 = IF RULES DON'T MAKE SENSE, YOU JUST DO YOUR OWN THING!
4 = SWEET NIBLETS! YOUR FREE-THINKING, RULE-BREAKING WAYS ARE OUT OF THIS WORLD! THERE'S NO FOOLING YOU, IS THERE? YOU'RE AN INDEPENDENT, GO-GETTER WHO WILL GO FAR. EXCELLENT WORK!

Nail art

Use these outlines to create nail designs fit for a pop princess!

Inspiration

Here are some of Hannah's favourite patterns to inspire you!

Quiz time

Do you know more about Miley than her own best friend?
Take this test to find out!

1) What's the name of Miley's brother?

a) Jacko ◯

a) Jakey ◯

a) Jackson ✓

2) Who wears this wig and why?

 lola-lilly so no one recenises her.

3) What's the name of Miley's best friend? Fill in the right circle!

Lilly ✓   Ashley

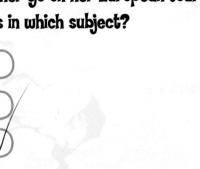

4) Miley's dad won't let her go on her European tour unless she gets good grades in which subject?

a) French ◯

b) Maths ◯

c) Biology ✓

5) Look at these shoes. Which ones belong to Miley?

a)    b)

✓

6) Can Lilly sing in tune?

a) Yes - she's great! ☐

b) No - she's terrible! ☑

7) Is Aunt Dolly Miley's real aunt?

a) Yes ☐

b) No ☑

8) Miley was embarrassed by her giant poster because...

a) Her hair looked bad! ☐

b) There was a fake spot on it! ☑

c) Her name was spelt wrong! ☐

9) Look at these three hairstyle close-ups
and guess who they belong to!

a)   b)   c)

lilly   _miley_

10. Which one of these titles isn't a Hannah Montana song?

a) Who Said

b) I Got Nerve ✓

c) The Best Of Both Worlds

Puzzle

P16 Jackson alert

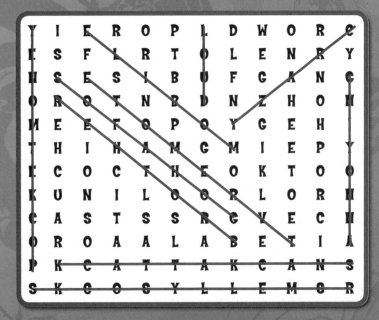

P20 Sketch suduko

P17 Funky fours

THE MYSTERY WORD IS... **HANNAH**

P37 Studio sound

66

answers

P44 Pop performance

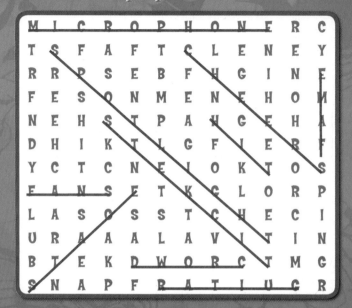

P50 Hannah's world

P45 Hanging out

P51 Matching pair

c and f are the
matching pair

Puzzle answers

P56 Criss cross

```
              H
              O
        O L I V E R
  C     L
L O C K E R
  O     I
  O   L I L L Y
  L   U
D E T E N T I O N         D
    R   C             N   O
S C H O O L   H O M E W O R K
    U   H             T   K
    B O O K S         E
    L
    E
```

P57 Guitar crazy

There are 80 guitars

P64 Quiz time

1) Jackson
2) Lilly – she's in disguise!
3) Lilly
4) Biology
5) The flip-flops
6) No – she's terrible!
7) No, she's her godmother.
8) There was a fake spot on it!
9) a-Lilly b-Oliver c-Robby
10) It's a trick question!
They are all Hannah
Montana songs!